Sea Nettles
New & Selected Poems

Sea Nettles
New & Selected Poems

Sue Ellen Thompson

GRAYSON BOOKS
West Hartford, Connecticut
graysonbooks.com

Sea Nettles: New & Selected Poems
Copyright © 2022 by Sue Ellen Thompson
Published by Grayson Books
West Hartford, Connecticut
ISBN: 978-1-7364168-5-3
Library of Congress Control Number: 2021950256

Interior & Cover Design by Cindy Stewart
Cover Image & Author Photo by Stuart Parnes

... the owl flew well beyond me
before I heard it coming, and when it
settled, the bough did not sway.

—Jane Kenyon, "Prognosis"

for Stuart, who feeds me

Acknowledgments

Bellevue Literary Review: "Global Warming"

Connecticut Review: "A Second Opinion," "Body English"

Connecticut River Review: "The Window Washers"

Delmarva Review: "How Friendship Dies"

Free State Review: "At 89, My Father Takes Up Swearing"

Freshwater: "July 17"

Inkwell: "Fast Food"

Kalliope: "Helping My Daughter Move into Her First Apartment"

Literature Today: "At the Dinner Table, 1961," "Genderqueer," "Landscaping During the Pandemic"

Little Patuxent Review: "Sharky's Dump"

Missouri Review: "Hospital Days"

Nimrod International Journal: "Letting Go," "The Blue Blanket," "In Praise of Cancer," "A Second Opinion," "No Children, No Pets," "Echo Rock," "London Wedding"

Poet Lore: "Inheritance"

Roads Taken: Contemporary Vermont Poetry: "Fernwood," "It was a small town"

Summerset Review: "My Father's Laundry"

The Talbot Spy: "Mid-Winter Migrants"

"Body English" also appeared in *Best American Poetry 2006.*

The following poems were read by Garrison Keillor on *The Writer's Almanac:* "The Blue Blanket," "11 Park Vista," "Sewing," "Leaning In," "Hospital Days," "Vegan."

"My Father's Laundry" won a Pushcart Prize and appeared in *Pushcart Prize XL: Best of the Small Presses.*

Contents

New Poems (2014-2021)

Selected Poems from *The Golden Hour* (2006)

Selected Poems from *They* (2014)

New Poems
(2014-2021)

The Universe

On the one whose family adores her, children and grandchildren,
the Universe bestows an incurable illness.

On the one who has been healthy all her life,
the Universe inflicts a financial crisis.

For the one who has always been well-to-do,
the Universe chooses not one unfaithful husband, but two.

To the one whose marriage has been long and happy,
the Universe grants a single child, estranged from his parents.

What does the successful mother have to lose?
The Universe thinks a premature death might do.

So do not bask in gratitude or relief
over what you have avoided or achieved.

It is not toward the expected that the Universe inclines.
For you, the Universe has something else in mind.

Genderqueer

Lapstrake, sprit-rigged,
our first boat had two
sets of oarlocks and a hole

in the forward thwart for a spar.
Enough room for the three
of us then, with my outstretched

leg as a whisker pole and astride
the mast our 12-year-old,
already at play with her balance.

The boat, which we soon
outgrew, made its way back
to the woman who'd built it.

But that child, who left
home at 22, never returned
as the child we knew.

We kept the tiller—carved
to resemble a woman's leg—
not to remind us of what

we thought she'd be,
but of the versatile,
small-boned craft in which,

had we seen the storm coming
and dropped the mast,
we might have rowed safely home.

Exchange Student, 1965

Inside the Bible's cover, in the spidery hand
of the organist, Mrs. Gore, known also
for her penmanship and for her skill
at a sewing machine: "Presented
to Sue Ellen Thompson by the Sunday School
of the First Baptist Church on the Eve
of Her Departure for Australia." Then,
a little farther down, a quote
from Joshua: "Be not afraid, neither
be thou dismayed: for the Lord thy God

is with thee withersoever thou goest."
I can see my mother, a sprig of holly
pinned to her winter coat, and my father
in his fedora as they drive me
to the airport, last night's fat mesh rollers
having coaxed my hair into a perfect flip.
But I am so afraid—having never
flown before or spent more than a night
away from them—that I leave

my jacket at the gate. Just as I convince
myself that I can live without my parents
for a year, just as I arrange my new skirt's
pleats beneath the seatbelt, my father comes
running down the aisle—surely to tell me
they've made a mistake in urging me
toward this adventure. But he holds up
the jacket that Mrs. Gore made, with its appliqué
of the continent toward which I'll soon be
on my way, without her god or anyone else's.

School Uniform

Wool serge, bottle green
with a yoke from which
three box pleats fell

like formal drapery.
The hemline had to graze
the floor when we knelt

at morning chapel.
Belted at the waist,
it formed a cave,

a secret place between
the blouse and tunic
where, at 17,

I kept his letters.
It was the year
I boarded at a school

for girls in Sydney,
and when I had to race
up from the cricket field

to get to History on time,
I often pressed a palm
against my chest

to make sure
not a word escaped
the window of an armhole.

It's a gesture I still
employ to reassure
a startled heart

or keep joy
in perspective.
But when I sold

the house I'd shared
with my husband
of 30 years, I found

the uniform hanging
in the cedar room, its dark
green faded by the light

from a narrow attic window.
And of its own accord,
my hand flew up

and clapped my chest
as if to keep that first
love safe in its hiding place.

Water View

A narrow strip
of grayish blue
just visible between
the sail loft and
what was a school
for the town's black children.

It barely changes color
with the seasons.
I rarely try to glimpse
it from my desk.
But on a day
when I wish things
were otherwise, it's there
I fix my gaze.

He had a dock,
a boat, a tree.
At sunset, it was like
a scene from a book
of Turner seascapes.
When it was time
for me to leave,
I took this bookmark
made of water.

Sea Nettles

Foolish wishes, passing
thoughts, dreams abandoned
long before they prove themselves

impractical. In mid-
July, the Chesapeake
is rife with them,

their coalescing forms
like memories struggling
to break the surface.

No matter how intense
the heat, we cannot risk
a hand trailed

in the sailboat's wake
or foot flung overboard
for cooling.

For each of us
there is a place,
a period of time,

a lover's face
that we must veer
away from—lest

what we thought
we had survived,
perhaps escaped,

graze us with its filaments,
set fire
to our skin and burn us.

Graduation Day, 2002

The cap and gown for which we'd paid
lay discarded back in her room,
although she'd cut two black strips
from the hem and wore them
as armbands. She'd pinned
two small silver wings to her back
and wore glasses with heavy frames
and no lenses.
                        When I look
at the photo now, 18 years later,
I wonder how I could have missed
what our child was trying to tell us:
that they were in mourning, had somewhere
to go, and could see what they had to
without any help from us.

Mid-Winter Migrants

When snow geese rise
en masse from a shallow pond.

When they wheel,
remembering what they left

behind, then wheel
again, a change of mind.

When one black wing-tip
clips that of another

and no one complains.
When they extend

their legs in front,
drawing their wings back

as if reluctant to land.
When they rise

again just moments later—
whether it's because

a car door slams
or in primordial alarm—

you can be certain
that they have no

choice and that they won't
return to this same pond

in this same company,
with this much hope.

Birding Instructor

Denim coverts sagging in the rear,
crest flattened and grooved by a baseball cap,
mantle hidden by the perforated mesh
of a binocular harness, he is patient
with our ignorance, advising us not
to scorn the frequent visitors
to our backyard feeders, but to master
the minutiae of their primaries and lores.
He never tires of pointing out the cardinals
and wrens we might otherwise dismiss—
the kind of man we should have married,
think those of us with an eye
not for what is transient or rare
but for the comforts of the common-
place. With us now, and here.

Tending My Husband's Eyebrows

Lying face-to-face with him in bed,
I tell him he should let me pluck

the white ones, which give him
an old man's unkempt look.

He squints and clenches while I
get to work—as if picking

at a machine-made hem,
hoping to find the one thread

the others will follow.
I should retire soon, he says,

thinking of friends who are already dead.
Some of the hairs turn in on themselves

like the insomniac's midnight dread.
Beyond the white sheet covering our bed,

beyond the white pillow framing his head,
a waist-deep snow, with another storm coming.

Fernwood

Dispatching the dead mandevilla leaves
with pendulum swings of my broom,
I am back on the paths of the wooded lot
next to my childhood home.

A third of an acre at most, it had trees
that cast a terrarium's jade
over the warren of rooms ringed with stones
where we squandered our summer days.

Connected by corridors paved with dirt
packed so hard it had the dull sheen
of wood, these chambers of wavering light
were the home of the house of our dreams.

My sisters and I swept them clean every day:
The minute a leaf drifted down,
we leapt upon it with rakes and brooms,
leaving only the bare, polished ground.

Day after day we swept the earth,
perfecting our shared domicile.
For whom? Our only visitors
were the cats who made it feel wild.

Our rage for order had less to do
with the home in which we'd been raised
than with our unconscious, unspoken wish
that our world continue unchanged.

What could go wrong here? Nothing, we thought.
But something disturbed that great calm:
Those summers, the side woods, our parents,
the cats—every one of them gone.

Journal: 1970-77

—in memoriam Frank A. Williams, Jr. (1949-77)

I'm reading the journal
I kept in my twenties.
The word "soul," like salt,
gets used every day.
It's good to remember

how I once lived in a body—
the smell of singed hair
and scorched flannel
from lying too close
to the fire. Something drew me

to the back of this closet:
the shortcut I took last week
through the graveyard that bordered
my old college campus.
My feet took me straight

to the rose granite headstone
shrouded with lichens,
its message clear only to me.
On every page he tells me
it's over, but I have not learned

to let go. I hold him between
these blue covers, so he
can't drive off in a blizzard
to see his new girlfriend—so I,
cast aside, won't grow old.

The Crossing

Walking back to the house through the woods
with my parents, then in their late 60s,
we came to the mountain stream

separating our land from the neighbor's.
The stones we had used as a bridge in the past
were slick with snowmelt, and we hesitated,

trying to pick out the safest path
to the opposite bank. With the confidence
of a man who had just turned 40,

my husband hopped across the stream first,
extending a hand to my father, who brushed it aside
as he made his own, less certain crossing.

Cautious as always, I stepped where they'd
stepped, flapping my arms for balance.
Alone now, my mother studied the stones

wearing their ruffled white collars.
She thought of the baby she'd lost
in her thirties, that long-submerged memory

breaking the surface, then being pulled
under again. She thought about falling
in icy water, her hip or a shoulder

striking the stones. She glanced
at us, over there on our own,
and announced that she would take

the road and meet us back at the house.
My husband was already heading for home,
my father shrugged meekly and followed.

So this was how a woman grew old:
I watched her slowly retreat from the stream
before turning and doing the same.

Sharky's Dump, 1958

On the way home from Sunday School, our father
veered off on a dirt road ending at a dump
where wild pigs could be seen, rooting
through the garbage. The swamp surrounding it
had grown a greenish skin, and our mother—
who believed in God but would not trade
a morning alone in the house for anything—
had given us her old, chipped dinner plates
to skim across it. Not far away,

the local airstrip ended in an archipelago
of concrete. Distant Piper Cubs
and Cessna Bobcats idled lazily until,
like greenhead flies inspired by the scent
of horses, they suddenly accelerated
toward us. Our father, still in his thirties,
lay across the open tailgate
of the station wagon, smoking Winstons
as the planes' low bellies rolled over him.

This was where we wanted to be
on a Sunday morning—flying our plates
out over the swamp's unbroken
green, terrorizing the local pigs—
while our father, who hadn't flown a plane
since the war ended and he'd returned
from prison camp, ethereally thin,
watched a younger man, winged
and unencumbered, fade into smoke and silence.

Smoking

I never forgot my mother's anger
the day she went looking for gloves
and found cigarettes in my sister's
coat pocket. Or the time I got carsick
on the way home from church
and she made my father pull over
and stub his butt out on the curb.
When he and my aunts played cards
in the kitchen, she'd open the windows
and turn on a fan. And if he wanted
to smoke after work, he'd have to
do it outdoors.
                        After she died,
he told me that in their retirement years,
when they dined at The Red Blazer
on Friday nights, she would often smoke
one of his cigarettes after dinner.
I tried to imagine her slender fingers
holding aloft a Winston King,
or a lasso of smoke floating over
their heads after leaving her lips
as a perfect ring. I tried to imagine her
doing anything that wasn't done
expressly for us, even keeping secrets.
But knowing this one was enough.

Fried Rice

—in memoriam F.A.W.

Senior year we didn't have much
money, so on weekends, for a treat,
we'd go to the Chinese place in Burlington
that overlooked the storm-cloud gray
of Lake Champlain. We'd share
an order of pork fried rice,

along with the complimentary
tea, and pick at it luxuriously
with our chopsticks. The waiter
treated us with some disdain,
but I was too naïve to think
my boyfriend's skin had anything

to do with it. Why would the Chinese
care? But as it turned out, everyone did—
from the grocery clerk who slapped
her "Lane Closed" sign down on the conveyor
just in front of us to the driver of the semi
hauling hay through town who shouted,

"Boy, get outta here!" as we waited
at the crosswalk. It's been fifty years,
but I'd like the waiter at Lucky Chen's
to know how gracefully a young
black man could wield two
chopsticks in his slender fingers,

holding a single grain of rice
up to the garish, red-globed light
as if it were a precious gem before
bestowing it on me. After the accident,
we all chipped in and bought
a plot for him in the college cemetery.

We ordered up a granite stone,
which I still tend when visiting
my alma mater, scraping at the lichens
still trying to obscure his name
with a credit card bearing mine.

Widows' Wednesday

One fell over backward in his chair
after a martini and a winning hand of bridge.
Another swerved into a parking lot,
hand on the dashboard, a little dizzy.

Another was in a hospital bed—tethered
by tubing, afloat on a whooshing sound.
Another was in a kayak, alone at sea—
his body perfect, not a single wound.

Some widows bear their losses regally
while others can't suppress a raucous laugh.
I am their guest tonight, visiting
the valley through which each of them has passed:

Grief's lush foliage, its bitter scent,
its atmosphere of rank bewilderment.

In Common

Because my father feared my mother's cat,
who took up residence on her pillow
after she died and would not leave,
forcing him to sleep, fully clothed,
on the outer ten inches of mattress;
because he had names for him
like "bastich" and "the devil-cat";
because he'd slap the dish down
and back away quickly, as if he had
planted an explosive, it never occurred
to me that the cat would outlive
him as well, or how much the two

of them would have in common.
But now, when the cat's claws snag
the carpeted stairs because he won't let me
trim them, I hear my father cry,
"You're hurting me!" yanking his foot
from between my knees. And when I clean
the litter box, which the cat often misses,
I hear my father apologize, "I can't see
a damn thing in there." And when
the cat sits by his bowl expectantly,
I still hear my father say, "I'll have
another, as long as you're up."

Evidence

I.

Newly married, I proudly displayed
my china on the open-shelved hutch.
Platters, two covered casseroles,
a creamer and four demitasse cups.

While I was out shopping one day,
my husband nudged the hutch from the wall
to level it. He didn't empty it first:
Two of the platters fell.

Knowing I would be home soon,
he hid the shards in a drawer.
For reasons mysterious to this day,
I walked in the kitchen door

and, without unbuttoning my coat,
went straight to that drawer
and opened it. Was this what it meant
to be married, or did it mean more?

II.

When my brother was 13, he fell
through the ice on the pond across the street.
No one saw him haul himself to safety,
leaving one glove frozen to a root.

Slipping in through the basement, he hid
his wet clothes behind the washing machine,
where they remained until he left home
for college, miraculous as that seems.

III.

Before the closing, I walked
through the house one last time.
Gone was the loveseat across
from the fireplace, gone was the fire.

I used to love gazing the length
of that house: From my chair in the den,
I could see the kitchen three rooms away,
a view I'd never embrace again.

I'd been happy here for 34 years,
but now the evidence seemed so thin:
scuff marks where the highchair once sat,
a stain on the floor where the cat's dish had been.

Landscaping During the Pandemic

Outside the grocery store, a young
Amish girl in a pleated organdy cap
is selling masks sewn from scraps
of quilting fabric. I choose the one
covered in shamrocks, although none
has a fourth leaf for luck.

Shoppers roam the aisles like bandits,
their intentions concealed. Where bales
of toilet paper once towered
stand empty shelves littered with coupons.
The fortunate pass slowly, as if drawn
to the scene of a fatal accident.

A neighbor has just been released
from the hospital. Her husband died
two floors above her, a phone held close
to his face. Walking by their house,
I glance at the window where I last saw him
shaving, leaning forward in search of more light.

The landscapers arrive with their truck full of sod
to fill the scars left by repeated flooding.
They give each roll an encouraging kick—
as if what was needed could be supplied, as if
there weren't absences too deep to fill,
as if a new carpet could stop the next flood.

Naming the Lake

A scar now runs the length
of the yard, filled
with rainwater, refreshed
by tides, where the grass
has given up growing—a lush
swale when we first arrived
a decade ago, a verdant
no-man's-land between
our house and our neighbor's.
Then the water began
to rise, reversing its way
through the drainage pipe
from the bay. Its long,

irregular shape reminds me
of the lake that separates
northern Vermont from
New York State, but I'm
naming it after my brother,
a middle child whose pliant nature
inclined him to let events rise
around him. And although
he never did anything wrong—
beyond underestimating
the consequences of his inaction—
he lives, to this day, in the midst
of what rose and would not recede.

It was a small town

which made everything
that happened there look
huge. The holiday parades
were endless, coursing
through the streets
like floodwater.
Parties overflowed
as well, channeled
by the narrow chambers
of what had once been
watermen's modest houses.

Almost everyone who lived there
had been Somebody once.
Widowed now, or simply
retired, they inflicted
their formidable talents
on a one-room library
and small stone church.

In summer, when the town
sprayed weekly for mosquitoes
after midnight, those
who remembered it was Tuesday
and brought their pets indoors
talked of it the whole next day,
inviting praise for their vigilance,
while those who'd left
their windows open
quietly prepared to die.

Low-lying and surrounded
on three sides by water, it afforded
little opportunity for harsh words
to evaporate. Instead, they often pooled

into final severings. Small disagreements
took root in the flood-softened earth
and spread like trumpet vine, dividing
entire neighborhoods into plaintiffs
and defendants. Why would anyone,

you might ask, want
to live there? Because every year
there was a day in early summer
when the first *magnolia grandiflora*
bent down low, distributing
its fleshy bowls to the poor and hungry,
of whom there were none and all
were lost in its vast perfume.

How Friendship Dies

With a decision
never explained,
an apology unwritten.

With a lunch
reluctantly arranged.
With an admission.

With a cold & vicious rain
falling outside.
With a suspicion.

With a refrain—
It's not about you—
more like an affront.

With feigned
indifference, eyes
averted. With volition.

With words so blunt
they carry blame
all the way from youth

to now, and forty years
are washed away
without a tear.

Global Warming

This town will be gone
in 50 years but enough

of us are still living here
to guarantee that at least two

of us are feuding.
It's bad this time,

there's money involved
and I am friends

with both of them.
Meanwhile, another

high tide is eating me
out of yard and drive

and real estate is falling.
X held me up

when I was down
and normally I'd take

her side, but Y
has an unerring

moral compass.
I realize I must

decide: Sell now, before
the waters rise, or stay

right here until I die,
loyal to both the home

I chose and the waters
that rose against it.

Sleeping on It

That sand-grain
irritation, that
plastic price-tag thread

that eyelash in
the conversation, that
earbud in the bed

that bug-bite on
my ankle that
talked to me all night

that blackberry seed
between my teeth that
wouldn't turn off the light

that part of me
that lives to prove
I'm almost always right

seems to have slipped
its leash and wandered
off during the night

leaving me
to wonder
why I let it gnaw

on the marrow
of an evening
now forever gone.

After Our Grown Child Leaves

Forty years old, but there's no other word
for one who is neither daughter nor son.

The car pulls away in a turmoil of gravel.
The afternoon heat stays behind.

We drag two chaises under the trees
and pretend to read before falling asleep—

knowing that when we wake,
it will be to the peace that only

the pond visited by geese
who can't help disturbing it knows.

My Mother in Her Seventies

Something in her was taking
its leave. When I challenged her
on an author's name or a fine
point of grammar or usage,
rather than argue with me

she'd go back to folding the sheets,
as if the truth weren't worth pursuing.
She no longer reigned supreme
over family disputes, confining
her realm to the kitchen sink

while battles were fought at the table.
She still did the cooking, pulled
all the weeds, but something diminished
the light she released, like a shade
drawn down slowly on the bright stream

that spills from a window at midnight.
I wanted a mother who'd fight back
at me. But as I approach the age
she was then, I find myself only too ready
to yield to my own child's talent

for discord. And if I've contracted
my mother's disease, of which losing the urge
to stand up for myself is a symptom,
I've been right, as she was, often enough
to admit it isn't that thrilling.

The Handoff

After sitting us down in his office to say
that tumors had hidden themselves throughout
my mother's body, the doctor stood formally
and, hands on her shoulders, urged her
in my direction. I sensed his unburdening,
his role in our family's tragedy now clearly
approaching its end. From this point on,
it was up to me, so I led her out
of the chilled examining room to the fierce,
confined heat of the car. As I buckled her
into the passenger seat, she stared up
at me with a newborn's eyes, blank
with surprise at the sudden intrusion of daylight.

Nursing

The nursing bra's rigorous harness,
no rosettes or satin bows.

The rocker's prescriptive ladderback,
an antique you didn't choose.

The beanbag body that barely
extended from elbow to palm.

A routine that could be boring,
even painful at times.

But tell me the truth now:
Last night, as you carried

that slumped bag of trash
out to the curb, didn't you long

for the days when life
went everywhere you went—

when you could not lay your burden down?

Bra Talk

When my sisters and I were in our teens
the dinner table talk was all about bras—
the crucial role that underwires played,
the pros and cons of seamless cups,
and whether rhinestones or rosettes

should mark the place where the wires
met above our breastbones. My father
would be sitting there, eating meatloaf
with his salad fork or using the butter knife
to spread his ketchup, and instead of lecturing us

on how society would judge us by our manners,
my mother would be telling us about the sale
on Maidenform at Kresge's, or crediting
the proper bra for seeing her through five
pregnancies and endless years of nursing.

What my father thought of our obsession
was a mystery. But I won't forget the day
I came home from the outlet mall and he—
approaching 90 and eight years a widower—
asked me what I'd bought. Reluctantly,

I pulled three Bali Ultra-light Lace Minimizers
from my shopping bag. Then, to head off
his embarrassment, I added, "Buy two,
get one free"—to which he replied, "That
would have made your mother very happy."

At the Dinner Table, 1961

Short-tempered, stubborn, my sister
had worked her way beneath my mother's skin
and chose an undistinguished Tuesday evening
to push her over the not-quite-visible line

that marked the limit of her patience.
My mother stood up, grabbed the Etch-
A-Sketch, my sister's favorite toy,
and brought it down hard on her flaxen head.

Stunned speechless by the tiny beads
of mercury pinballing my sister's face,
the four of us stared at the shattered plastic—
still in its frame, but concave.

Had she lived as long as she wanted to,
my mother would be 91 today.
If you look at my sister's hair in the sunlight,
you'll see an undertone of silvery gray—

all that remains of her youthful obstinacy
and of our awe at how a mother under duress
could be so calm, so sure of what
needed doing. Facing her own death

forty-one years later, she turned away
the cups of water we held to her chin
and, reaching for what shocked and silenced us,
became what she had always been.

Power Failure

At first it's an adventure, following
a flashlight beam down to the frigid,
furling stream and hauling back
a bucketful for flushing. A candlelit
supper, fueled by confidence
that the fridge will soon start humming.

Morning and the sky's so dark
it looks as if a woolen scarf
is draped across the sun's
pale lampshade. Patience stretches
thin. The trees are black cords
dangling from the sky. In his final years,

my widowed father would not leave
his freezing house, the bed with half
its covers tucked in, three days into
an outage. He let the cold and dark
move in—he held his arms out
to his new companions.

Napping

Six months retired, my husband
has started napping with me on the daybed
in my office over the garage. I buzz him
on the intercom around 2:30, when I feel

my afternoon doziness coming on.
The back door wheezes as he leaves
the house, a book under his arm.

We lie head-to-foot on the twin mattress,
purchased in the hope that it would lure
our grown child for a visit, and sink
beneath the duvet, unable to see

each other's face beyond
the tented mountains
and the books pitched at their base.

Soon one of us, and then the other,
puts the book aside, rolls over
on a hip and shoulder.
Like the sterling salad forks—

indispensable at dinner parties
when we were young but now relegated
to a felt-lined box in berths

facing opposite ways—we don't know if
or when we'll be of use to anyone
beyond each other again.
So, with one foot planted firmly

in the warm earth of the other's armpit,
we let the afternoon close over us,
we grow accustomed to our narrow space.

Birding at Bombay Hook
National Wildlife Refuge

Snow geese in the thousands quilt
the pond at Bombay Hook. At a sound
inaudible to us, they rise in sudden

undulations—a blanket shaken out,
allowed to settle. They talk
about the weather and the next stop

on their journey north in voices loud
enough to carry all the way
to the parking lot. As I eavesdrop

from the viewing tower, waiting for
the next alarm, a C-17 lumbers
across the sky on its way to Dover Air Base.

I recognize it as the plane
that brings the flag-wrapped coffins
home from Afghanistan. The gossiping

continues, but my binoculars are trained
on the upward-sloping aft ramp door—the one
that drops down slowly, like a jaw.

Spring in New Hampshire

Toward the end of his life, my father
stopped watching DVDs, complaining
that everyone mumbled. He lost patience
with the news on TV, a ritual
that had accompanied his nightly
manhattan. He had to stop buying
his own groceries when his car
started coming home injured.
Snow, which he loved, was a danger
now, too, so he stayed indoors from November
to May as it filled the yard like a silo.

One April day, black patches appeared
in the thick gray ice of the driveway.
The temperature soared to 75,
so I brought him outside in his bathrobe.
On a plastic chaise I dragged down
from the barn, he sunned himself
like an old polar bear. What
did he dream of? Climbing

the now-forbidden stairs to the second floor,
and from there, through a narrow hatch
at the back of a closet, out to the shed roof,
from which he could see, with his old
pilot's eyes, the top of Mt. Kearsarge.

The Nest

—for Eileen and Terry

Just out of the hospital,
he can't have wine, or the pale slabs
of cheese I've arranged
like a winning hand of solitaire.
He's brought his own blood
orange soda, asks glumly for ice.

His wife moves the chips
another inch out of his reach.
Her features still have their fine,
flared edge, but fear of losing him
has made their beauty more difficult
to admire, like the silver serving dish,
its surface battered by knives.

She watches him raise
a celery stick to his mouth—
as alert to whatever the next
breath might bring as the osprey
who, gazing fiercely into the wind,
guards what looks like storm debris
but is someone's beloved home.

Naming the Birds

My husband calls anything with vast,
fringed wings a vulture, anything
that flits from tree to tree a sparrow,
and whatever descends upon a pond
en masse a Canada goose. All ducks
are mallards, and the song
that emanates from hedge or bush
must be that of a mockingbird.

The rare, the migratory simply don't
exist—because if they did,
it would mean the unexpected
circling our little patch of peace and green:
the two of us at 70, staring at the sky
with mouths agape, the shadow
that of neither hawk nor eagle.

The Window Washers

Autumn meant that it was time to wash the windows,
my father on a ladder pitched to clear the shrubs,
my mother clutching her rags and spray-bottle—
her face stern, like a judge's.

The only sound was tapping on the glass:
Not my side, must be yours. Starting
in the west so they could dodge the sun,
they'd clear the smirch of woodsmoke, summer rain.

Last was the window over the screened porch,
positioned where a ladder couldn't reach.
My mother, in her 70s, would balance
one foot on an antique Hitchcock chair

and raise the other, as if hurdling the sill,
then fold her torso gracefully in half
before emerging on the mossy shingles. Back
turned as he lugged the ladder to the barn,

my father barely registered the *thunk*
of sash on frame that meant her job
was finished—never worrying about her
falling; like most men, thinking he'd fall first.

The Day After the Funeral

Because my husband left the day before
with my car keys in his pocket, and FedEx
won't deliver until late afternoon,
my sister takes a taxi to the airport
while I wait in my father's house, alone.

I stretch out on the canopy bed where both
my parents died. Gone are the inhalers,
the reading glasses, the penlight and the pills,
the eye drops, Kleenex, paperbacks,
the magnifying mirror, plastic urinal.

Their photos stare just past each other
on the bureau, as if scanning
a crowd of strangers without success.
I lie perpendicular to the gentle swales
their bodies have left in the mattress.

Grief has abandoned its topmost perch,
and I am a tree stripped bare of foliage
and birdsong, a latticework of air
through which thought tumbles freely
without catching anywhere.

My mother walked briskly
toward her death a decade ago.
Now my father, knotted and bent,
has finally caught up with her, grabbing
her sleeve to get her attention.

One day I will follow them
into my own absence,
but for now, I stay behind:
my life at an angle to theirs,
their shapes slowly yielding to mine.

London Wedding

Held beneath the withering gaze
of the Woolwich Town Hall's
marble Queen Victoria, it was
a small, mid-week affair,
attended only by my boyfriend's
co-workers, looking for an excuse
to knock off early. Afterward,

we gathered at a local wine bar,
where we ordered burgers
and the Nouveau Beaujolais.
It was raining as we walked home
to our flat along the busy Trafalgar Road,
a bent umbrella rib channeling water
down our backs. He slipped his hand

between the buttons of my raincoat
and held it there against the small,
defiant seed of what would one day be
our greatest challenge. A car swerved
suddenly to avoid a hazard we couldn't
see. A siren wailed; a child screamed.
But at 31, alone together on a dark,
wet street in a city that barely knew us,
I don't remember being anything but happy.

Selected Poems

from

The Golden Hour

(2006)

In Praise of Cancer

For giving her those first six weeks
of summer, doing crosswords on the porch
in a kimono worn so thin the morning light

and birdsong could move through it. For drowsy
afternoons in chemo, reading magazines,
and for the nurses who could slip a needle

underneath the paper of her skin as easily
as a lover's name into a conversation.
For allowing us to see her as a girl again,

a stringbean, then a downy-headed infant,
curling in upon herself for sleep, and finally
as something luminous, desiring. For sending us

the unseasonable snow that dawdled
in the autumn foliage the day we drove
through the White Mountains past

Robert Frost's house, pausing long enough
for her to say, *And that has made all
the difference.* For the afternoon I brought her

home, exhausted, from the hospital and laid
her down to nap on that same porch—
the screens dissolving now in late

October's radiance—and for the sleep
she sank into so gratefully a smile
shone like water on her thin, dry lips.

For taking what it had to take so casually
at first—an appetite for olives, windfall
hair. For being quick and greedy at the end.

My Father Gets His Wish

For years my father had longed to be
like the men he'd seen in the ads on TV,
recumbent in their La-Z-Boy recliners.
He'd tell my mother in all honesty

there were few things that could make
an old man happy. With that, he'd slink
off to the living room, which was arranged
exactly like the one she'd seen

in *Country Living*, with wing chairs anchoring
a reproduction oriental and a Queen
Anne coffee table tiled with magazines.
After our first visit from Hospice,

when my mother found out she'd have to rearrange
her bedroom furniture to accommodate
the hospital bed she'd sworn would never take
the place of her canopied, pencil-post antique,

she said that when his birthday came,
I should buy my father a recliner. She
had begun to see our lives continuing
without her, and she wanted them to be

just like the old lives, but blessed by everything
to which she'd been an obstacle. As she signed
the check, I watched the horses from the neighboring
farm raise their fluent heads as one

and, summoned by the invisible, move in unison
towards an opening in the pasture fence,
while a brisk wind closed the gate behind them.

11 Park Vista

We rented a room from an English violinist
and shared the kitchen that filled the second floor.
We had until the lessons downstairs were finished
to cook and eat our dinner before

he started his. Married now
and beginning to show, I took the train
to London every day and joined the crowd
perched on folding campstools at the Tate.

Returning one evening, I saw my husband
wreathed in steam above the kitchen stove
while a young girl raised her violin
and released a flock of sparrows in the parlor below.

I paused on the front walk, breathless with greed.
Food, music, children—all within reach.

Fast Food

When the doctor prescribed a liquid called Megace,
designed to elicit an appetite where hers
had waned to a crescent, it made my mother crave
the foods she'd spent a lifetime avoiding.
She'd lift the lid and start licking her fingers
before we had cleared the parking lot
at Kentucky Fried Chicken, and once
she made me drive straight from her CAT scan
to Burger King, where she downed a Whopper
with extra cheese and more delight
than she'd ever displayed at Thanksgiving.
After raising a shake made with real
ice cream to her face, she closed
her eyes reverently and shaved her moustache
with a finger. On our way home from chemotherapy,

she made me stop at McDonald's for lunch,
and with the same bliss-driven spiritedness
said she wanted a picnic. The sky had been lowering
its hopes all day, but we found a grassy place
on the banks of the Merrimack. Propped
by a damp stone, lichen-stained, she devoured
her paper-wrapped feast. Her hair—
which would fall like the leaves of the willow
behind her in just one week—caught the mist
that rose like a thought of rain in the mind of the heavens.
It formed a loose cloud around her face,
bathed in silvery pleasure. She held
a crisp sickle of fry aloft and gazed
at its tip, dripping in rich red ketchup.
What could be better than this? she asked,
and indeed, I could think of nothing.

Sewing

The night before my older sister's wedding,
my mother and I sat up late
hand-stitching a little cloud of netting
to the brim of each bridesmaid's hat.

To be alone with her was so rare
I couldn't think of what I had to say.
We worked in silence beneath the chandelier
until it was almost daybreak.

Soon I'd have a room of my own
and she would only be cooking for six.
We drifted among the wreaths we had sewn,
nursing quietly on our fingertips.

That she still had me was a comfort,
I think. And I still had her.

Five Kids

My mother claimed she could tell us apart
by the sound of our peeing. Lying in bed, she knew
my older sister's bossy gush, the spurts
of impatience from my younger sister, the altitude-

induced tonal differences of the two boys.
She said my pee was tentative
and ladylike, something I enjoyed
hearing because I was neither. If I was sick

in the middle of the night and cried out "Mom!"
at the crescendo of my retching—something I still do,
in my head—she'd be at my side already, with her "I'm
here, honey" and the right toothbrush.

As for my only child, my daughter?
I think I don't know half as much about her.

A Second Opinion

Because none of them had touched her yet—
aside from the random palm laid flat
upon her tumored abdomen—
when Doctor Meadows made a D-ring
with his hand around my mother's wrist
she fell for him, no matter that her first
impression had been of someone slightly
vain, his crossed leg in its dress sock
descending to a graceful arch,
his narrow foot like mangrove rising
from the marsh of an Italian loafer.
He reached across the corner of his desk,
and with one finger on the porcelain knob
of her wrist bone, rubbed his thumb
against the current of her racing pulse.

You realize, Mrs. Thompson, this disease
will take your life, he said, to which
my mother murmured *Yes*
in the rapt and breathless way
that women have when men who are beyond
their wildest dreams decide to pay
them some attention. Observing this,
I understood what *bedside manner* means,
and for the first time thought of it
as having to do not so much with kindness
as with a willingness to be
here at this place of immense and frightening delicacy.

Wallpapering

My parents argued over wallpaper. Would stripes
make the room look larger? He
would measure, cut, and paste; she'd swipe
the flaws out with her brush. Once it was properly

hung, doubt would set in. Would the floral
have been a better choice? Then it would grow
until she was certain: It had to go. Divorce
terrified me as a child. I didn't know

what led to it, but I had my suspicions.
The stripes came down. Up went
the flowers. Eventually it became my definition
of marriage: bad choices, arguments

whose victors time refused to tell,
but everything done together and done well.

Hospital Days

The tests, the bloodwork—they
were good days, with magazines
to absorb the time spent waiting.
The nurses' banter spread a sheen
of normalcy over everything,
and the doctors left a little space
in their advice where spirit
might lodge. The three of us
went everywhere together, and at last
I knew the pleasure that the only child
takes in the company of her makers.

Then the doctor came to us one day
and said the chemo hadn't made
the kind of progress he was looking for,
that we could take my mother home
and stay. We sat there, stunned by what
our weeks of rushing to appointments
had not left us time to contemplate,
then drove home without speaking. This day,
unlike the others, would not end
with smiles and good-byes, my father's
and my arms tucked beneath my mother's
and hope's modest, steady flame
still unextinguished in us at the thought
of eating supper at the kitchen table
before we called the cats in from the dark.

Letting Go

Throughout my mother's illness, friends
kept telling me that when her time came,
she would need permission from me to depart
for the vast white snows of death.

So I drove north frantically that final night,
great gulps of highway disappearing
down the station wagon's open throat,
arriving not to uniforms and flashing lights

but to a house so nearly dark I thought
she might have tired of waiting. A single
small lamp struggled in the farthest corner
of the room, its gaunt light faltering

just inches from the thick, cut-paper
shade. I climbed in bed with her and listened
as my own quick breathing calmed,
then hers did, just before it tapered

to a halt. Years ago I'd gone home, spurned
by a lover she never knew I'd had. She fed me,
washed my clothes, while I drew closer to my own
despair. She didn't have to say a word.

Leaning In

Sometimes, in the middle of a crowded store on a Saturday
afternoon, my husband will rest his hand
on my neck, or on the soft flesh belted at my waist,
and pull me to him. I understand

his question: Why are we so fortunate
when all around us, friends are falling prey
to divorce and illness? It seems intemperate
to celebrate in a more conspicuous way

so we just stand there, leaning in
to one another, until that moment
of sheer blessedness dissolves and our skin,
which has been touching, cools and relents,

settling back into our separate skeletons
as we head toward Housewares to resume our errands.

Body English

I'd seen a golfer's body curve
into a deep parenthesis as the ball
inched toward the cup, and I knew
how mothers in the bleachers leaned
and flapped their useless wings
when their child's kick arced perfectly
before descending shy of the goal.
As the two men from the funeral home
maneuvered my mother's body
through the narrow, sloping hallways
of her eighteenth-century cape
to where the black van had reversed its way
up the steep slope to the porch,
I cowered with my father and my sister
in a distant bedroom, waiting
for their footsteps and the thumps
against the woodwork to abate.
Through a narrow opening in the door
that centuries of weather had warped
so that the latch no longer fit,
we glimpsed the stretcher as they carried it
across the porch. *Alley-oop!* one said
as the other raised my mother's bare feet
high, letting her head, so newly sprouted
with winter wheat, tilt dangerously
downward. Suddenly the three of us
were on our feet—bodies craned,
chins lifted skyward—as if by pitching
all our weight, we could prevent
the next bad thing from happening.

Helping My Daughter Move into Her First Apartment

This is all I am to her now:
a pair of legs in running shoes,

two arms strung with braided wire.
She heaves a carton sagging with CDs

at me and I accept it gladly, lifting
with my legs, not bending over,

raising each foot high enough
to clear the step. Fortunate to be

of any use to her at all,
I wrestle, stooped and single-handed,

with her mattress in the stairwell,
saying nothing as it pins me,

sweating, to the wall. Vacuum cleaner,
spiny cactus, five-pound sacks

of rice and lentils slumped
against my heart: up one flight

of stairs and then another,
down again with nothing in my arms.

No Children, No Pets

I bring the cat's body home from the vet's
in a running-shoe box held shut
with elastic bands. Then I clean
the corners where she has eaten and
slept, scrubbing the hard bits of food
from the baseboard, dumping the litter
and blasting the pan with a hose. The plastic
dishes I hide in the basement, the pee-
soaked towel I put in the trash. I put
the catnip mouse in the box and I put
the box away, too, in a deep
dirt drawer in the earth.

When the death-energy leaves me,
I go to the room where my daughter slept
in nursery school, grammar school, high school,
I lie on her milky bedspread and think
of the day I left her at college, how nothing
could keep me from gouging the melted candle-wax
out from between her floorboards,
or taking a razor blade to the decal
that said to the firemen, *Break
this window first.* I close my eyes now
and enter a place that's clearly
expecting me, swaddled in loss
and then losing that, too, as I move
from room to bone-white room
in the house of the rest of my life.

Napping

My mother, who had walked six miles,
six days a week for years, knew
that her life was ending. One day she smiled
at me and said, "I'm not in the mood

for walking today. I think I'll take
a nap instead." She never napped
before lunch. But how else could she say
it? All morning she lay wrapped

in an afghan on the sofa, her eyes intent
upon a pattern taking shape in the air.
I cleaned her kitchen, my diligence
a substitute for grieving and a kind of prayer.

She didn't tell me not to: adrift, serene,
quietly dropping the reins of her routine.

Vegan

My daughter hauls her sacks of beans
and vegetables in from the car and begins to chop.
My father, who has had enough caffeine,
makes himself a manhattan-on-the-rocks.

It's Sunday, his night for sausage and eggs,
hers for stir-fried lentils, rice, and kale.
Watching her cook eases his fatigue
and loneliness. Later, she'll trim his toenails.

He no longer has an appetite
for anything beyond this evening ritual.
But he'll fry himself an egg tonight
and eat dinner with his granddaughter. For a widower,

there is no greater comfort in the world
than his girls and his girls' girls.

The Blue Blanket

Toward the end, my father argued
with my mother over everything: He wanted
her to eat again. He wanted her to take

her medicine. He wanted her
to live. He argued with her in their bed
at naptime. He was cold, he said,

tugging at the blanket tangled
in my mother's wasted limbs. From the hall
outside their room I listened

as love, caught and fettered, howled
at its captors, gnawing at its own flesh
in its frenzy to escape. Then I entered

without knocking, freed the blanket
trapped between my mother's knees and shook
it out once, high above

their bodies' cursive. It floated
for a moment, blue as the Italian sky
into which my father flew his bombs

in 1943, blue as the hat I'd bought her
for the winter she would never live
to see. My father's agitation eased,

my mother smiled up at me, her face
lucent with gratitude, as the blanket
sifted down on them like earth.

Selected Poems
from
They
(2014)

A Photograph of My Daughter at 9

She's sitting in a dining room chair.
Light through the blinds has tightened
its straps across her narrow body
and a blow dryer has transformed
her wispy hair into a child-sized helmet.
Her legs are crossed and shackled
to each other at the ankle and she grips
the chair arms with the wild-eyed stare
of one who is about to undertake a journey
full of risk and turbulence instead of a simple meal.

A Comfort

When she turned six and wouldn't wear
a dress to her own party,

the other mothers smiled knowingly
and said, "She'll come around."

When she was ten and threw away
the valentine a boy had sent,

my mother said, "She's only ten.
She'll come around." At twelve,

she wore her father's flannel shirts
to school. "They call it grunge,"

her teacher said. "She'll come around
when she's a little older."

In high school, there were other girls
who spiked their hair and dyed

it dark magenta, but only mine
wore underwear designed for men

beneath her low-slung cargo pants.
Waiting outside the school one day,

I heard another mother say,
"I know my daughter won't look

like this forever. When she goes
to college, she'll come around." Then

she added, with some embarrassment,
"So will yours." I shook my head.

My daughter had worn camouflage
to nursery school. She came home

from college with piercings in her cartilage.
"Stop worrying," my husband said.

"She'll come around when she has to get
a job." I knew that would make

no difference. She found a place
that hired her just as she was.

"She'll meet a guy and that will be
the end of it"—more than a few

friends told me this. "You
don't know my daughter,"

I said. But cradling myself in bed,
I thought, *She'll come around.*

The Empty House

House that we bought just a month before
we were married; after the wedding, the rooms
unfolded anew. House where I brought

the baby straight from the hospital, sat
at the dining room table, unbuttoned my blouse.
House of the Christmas Eve dinners,

my niece and her boyfriend together
on the piano bench, which to this day
bears a mark from the heat of their thighs.

House of the homework assignments, the three of us
up half the night making two-inch-tall tepees
of bark from the birch tree and little plaid bedrolls

cut from an old flannel shirt. House
so toxic with anger, a teenager's
venomous mouth, that for three years

we dared not have anyone over for dinner.
Then, when she left us for college,
a silence so vast

we inflicted our surplus endearments
on a long-suffering 12-year-old cat.
House of near-human sounds—

bone-creaks and moaning, sighing and wailing
in storms. House of our long years of marriage,
your limbs entwined around mine

like ivy around the round stones
of the stone walls surrounding the yard.
House of the woodpile, the woodshed,

the canvas wood carrier carried
six times a day from the shed
to the wood stove, the smell of felled maple

and oak. House I came home to
after my mother died, put down
my suitcase and lay on the bed

with my coat still on, hands
folded over the knot of my sorrow
as sleep closed its massive green door.

Postcards

Postmarked Ann Arbor, Fort Wayne,
Memphis, and a dozen other places
I never knew she'd visited,
my daughter's postcards
to her widowed grandfather
were the only way I had of finding out
what she was up to during those years
when her phone calls thinned
to almost nothing. He would leave them
on the nightstand in the bedroom
where I slept when I was visiting,
and I would read them—row
after row of minuscule block letters
pausing patiently before the fenced-off plot
she'd set aside for sheltering his name
and address—just before I went to sleep.
She often signed them, "Thinking
of you, Pop," and I did not for one minute
doubt which shelf he occupied
in the library of her affections.

"And how did that make you,
her mother, feel?" a shrink
would no doubt ask, and I
would have to answer
that it made me happy—happier,
I think, than if those cards had been addressed
to me. Here was a man who'd waited
19 years for a grandson, who had kept
his wishes silent as six granddaughters
were born. Here was a man
who liked to spend a summer day

fishing lazily along the Merrimack,
winter weekends stacking cordwood,

and here was a child who wanted to be
at his side, doing what he did. They seemed
to have an understanding: She would give him
all the love that she could spare
for generations preceding her own
and in return, he'd never say a word
about her tattoos or her piercings
or her boyish haircut, or ask her why
she hid her breasts and let
her mustache show. He would simply think
of her as the grandson he'd been waiting for,
and she would always think of him
as the man she wanted to be like
when she was old and had
no grandson of her own.

Postcard: Lakota Wolf Preserve, Columbia, NJ

Hey Pop! I went on a 24-hour getaway
with some friends to the Delaware Water Gap,
two hours north of Philly. We floated down
the river in tubes all afternoon, camped
for the night, then got up early
for the "wolf watch" at a place nearby
where 25 timber, tundra, and arctic wolves
now live. There were bobcats, who'd been someone's pets,
and two red foxes. All were either born
in captivity or rescued from roadside attractions,
so they weren't afraid of humans. I was thinking
about that cougar you once spotted
in New Hampshire. Next time you see him,
tell him there's a home for him here in New Jersey—
isn't that where you spent your "wild youth"?
I miss our early morning walks. Love, Thomasin.

At 89, My Father Takes Up Swearing

The army must have taught him how,
and then he spent those two-and-a-half years
in a German P.O.W. camp, with all
the other starving men who used
such words to salt the watery gruel

of their existence. But when he came back
to my mother, she would not permit
a "damn" or "hell" or any of those in-vain names
to cross her well-scrubbed doorsill. He never
slipped in the more than 50 years

I listened. But now that she's beneath the lawn
of the cemetery on the other side of town,
he cannot find his fucking cane—the one
that is no goddamned good for anything
because the rubber tip keeps falling

off. Jesus, what a fucking pain
to bend and search for it beneath his bed,
especially when he hits his head
on the open drawer of that bedside
fucking table. He lies there on the threadbare rug

and tries to remember what the hell it was
he lost. My mother, were she still
alive, would flush in anger and cut him off.
But who am I—who have not leapt
from a burning plane or slept in a barracks

whose floorboards must be taken up,
one at a time, for burning when the coal
runs out—to tell my father what to say?
Where the fuck is his goddamned cane?
Shit, man—I have no idea.

Postcard: Ocean City, New Jersey

Hey Pop! It was unbearably hot
and humid in Philly today,
so my housemates and I headed out
to the good old Jersey shore—not far
from where you said you used to take
your station wagon full of kids
when they were young. We picnicked,
swam, and napped all afternoon.
Then, at sunset, we shared a bucket
of curly fries and watched a bunch
of little girls rehearsing for a dance recital
in the theater on the boardwalk. So many
chubby legs in shiny pants and tutus!
So many sparkly eyelids and fake ponytails!
So many stage moms! It made me think
of my rich New Jersey heritage—and that,
of course, means you. Love, Thomasin.

They

Reading "About the Artist" at my daughter's first
solo exhibit, I notice that she refers
to herself as "queer"—a once derogatory word
that is now back in vogue. Unversed

in the linguistic proprieties, I read
on, hoping to unearth some clue
as to the exact nature of her gender-identity view
of herself, and this is what I see:

"Their work is characterized by the play
of the familiar and the unfamiliar, made from objects
they have found within a five-block
radius of their apartment." Who is *they?*

Does she have a partner I've not met—
a co-creator I know nothing about?
Because my experience with "coming out"
is limited to a gay friend from college, she sets

me straight: Since neither "he" nor "she"
is accurate, I should refer to her as "they."
Whether or not I'm okay
with this is irrelevant. If I want to see

her more than once a year, I may
as well begin by unlearning the rule
of noun-pronoun agreement. In this school,
I am the student; she, the teacher. *They.*

Echo Rock

When my daughter was young, my father
built a hut for her on Echo Rock,
the granite mound for which the farm
was named and from which, if she faced
the house, she could pitch her name
and have it flung right back. Made
from barn board scraps the weathered gray
that characterized the foreshortened days
of a New Hampshire winter, it had a single
window facing north and a door that she could padlock.

I hear her still, from the clump of underbrush
that kept her refuge and its secrets hidden,
at the end of a day when it appeared
that she had played contentedly alone.
"Thomasin!" she called repeatedly,
as if there were another of her
and it was time now for them both to hurry home.

Homemade Postcard

Hey Pop—It's been snowy and cold
this week in Philly, but I've been enjoying
the flickering "flames" of my new
plug-in "woodstove." It brings a little
New Hampshire charm to my big city life—
I just come home and flick it on
for instant coziness and ambiance.
Speaking of comforts, I read an article
in the New York Times about some bees
in Brooklyn whose "honey stomachs" turned
bright red and who produced red honey.
It seems that they'd been gathering
their nectar at a nearby maraschino
cherry factory. That made me think of you
and your manhattans. You always say
the cherry at the bottom is your favorite part.
Be careful: I don't want your insides
turning red! Remember what the doctor said:
Drink more water. Love, Thomasin.

My Father's Laundry

When my mother died, my father discovered
he could not fold a fitted sheet. Patiently,
I showed him the appropriate technique,
but in the months, then years, that followed,
I would find the bottom sheets he'd laundered
spread out on the guest room bed,
where they remained until one
of his three daughters came to visit.

He could operate the washing machine, the dryer,
he could roll a pair of socks until one
disappeared inside the other,
but those fitted sheets defeated him—
or else that bedroom was the place
he went to say, *I can't do this without you.*

July 17

On a wooden chaise by the water's edge
I dozed and read, dozed and read,
forgetting that my mother was dead,
that my daughter had decided she was a man,
and that I was living apart from my husband.
I was reading a book I'd already read,
which made it easier to put aside,
which made it easier to close my eyes
and dismiss my own misfortunes.

The wind lifted the heads of grasses
bowed by the heat, like forgotten wishes
revived by memory, then left them listless
again. I did the same: One
by one, I summoned my obsessions,
then waved them off. A restless
bee nursed on the clover beneath my feet,
but I let this sweetness elude me.
For hours that seamless afternoon

I drifted, so far from familiar shores,
it was as if I'd fallen overboard
and no one noticed. My reward
was respite from both fear and dread
but also from joy. It was a kind of death,
this sleep: I was a chord
struck once, dissipating in the summer air.
I awoke to my neighbor, in her yard somewhere,
calling, "Shadow! Shadow!" Nothing more.

At the Kitchen Window

Ignoring the tattoos, the piercings, the triangle of hair
shaved off geometrically above each ear,
the elastic waistband of men's underwear
visible above her belt (which cut across her rear

the way my mother's tape measure did
when I was her age and took my measurements),
my father always welcomed visits
from my daughter, which were more frequent

than her visits home. She'd sit with him on the porch
in the evenings, praising his tomatoes, asking questions
about what it was like to be a pilot or a prisoner of war.
He never said anything to anyone

indicating he was bothered by the way she looked—
except that morning when he stood
at the kitchen window, watching as she took
aim, pitching windfall apples into the woods

that fringed his vast, well-cared-for yard,
and said, "If I didn't know differently,
I'd think she was a boy." I poured
some coffee I didn't want or need

into a mug as slowly as I could,
and then some milk, and stirred.
I waited for that thought, and the mood
it cast over me, to settle without a word.

"I Love Women"

My father said this to the tall, blond ophthalmologist
who greeted him as he was wheeled into the operating room
where she would give him back his vision. He said it
to the caretaker who tucked him in at night, although he told me
privately that she could "stand to lose a few." He said it
to the stranger in the parking lot at Shaw's, whose head
was pulled so far back in her parka hood that she grabbed
his arm and pulled him close, thinking he was her husband.
He even said it to his grown, transgender grandchild,
who laughed and took it all in stride. Less than a week
before he died, as I leaned across his bed to rearrange
the blankets, he hauled his good arm back
and swatted me on the ass—a gesture that must have cost
what little strength he had. "Pop!" I said, in a voice
I hoped would combine the amused surprise
and muted moral outrage that had characterized
my mother's reply each time he grabbed a handful
of her not-so-youthful flesh, "What are you doing?"
He let his head fall back into the pillow's ample lap
as a smile suffused his ancient face. "Sue, you're looking
good," he said. "In fact, you're looking great."

The Last Time I Saw My Father

He couldn't sleep, couldn't get comfortable
in the hospital bed we'd brought
into his room, would push a button
and his feet would rise up to the ceiling.
He had no appetite, he was thirsty
but drinking only made him want to pee
and he couldn't do that, either. In the middle
of the night, I found him sitting
with his thin legs dangling
off the bed, pajama bottoms
halfway to his knees, one hand holding
what I didn't want to see, the plastic urinal
tipped over on the table, out of reach.

With sudden clarity, he looked at me
and asked, "Are we drilling today?"
I thought he might be dreaming
about the V.A. dental clinic, where he
had endured six decades of extractions,
root canals, and a series of bridges that never
seemed to work or fit—the legacy
of his stay in a German P.O.W. camp.
But then I realized that it was 1943
and he was back in Lubbock, Texas,
in the Army Air Corps. "No drills today,"
I told him, and this seemed to comfort him.
"Good," he said, and then, "I'm tired,"
closing his eyes as if he knew
that nothing further would be required.

Postcard: Wild Turkeys,
Pocomoke River State Park

Dear Pop: We didn't see any wild
turkeys here, but there were turkey hunters
everywhere. I took an evening walk
to the clearing near our campsite
that reminded me of our "deer walks"
after dinner in New Hampshire—
that same sensation of stepping through
thick grass on a full stomach.
I love places where I can walk alone
at dusk and not be frightened—
hard to come by in the city.

Anyway, I'm sorry to hear
you've been in too much pain
to sleep these past few weeks.
Maybe you should try
thinking about the hunting trips
you used to take when you were young.
I love and miss you, Thomasin.

Inheritance

After the funeral, I told my daughter
she could choose what she wanted
from her grandfather's New Hampshire farmhouse.
She took the yellowed handkerchiefs
with which he'd wiped his brow
when mowing the lawn those 30 summers
after his retirement; a leather belt,
well-worn but stiff from hanging
where he'd abandoned it when nothing
but suspenders could keep his pants
from falling off his ancient hips;
and the pajama bottoms he had worn
for what turned out to be
his last eight days and nights.

As I watched her fold and pack
her small inheritance in a grocery bag,
I asked, "Isn't there something else?"
thinking of a rug or piece of furniture.
She went directly to the small spice chest
that had hung on the wall for fifty years.
Opening each of the miniature drawers
and peering inside, she said, "Just this"
and pulled out a campaign-style button
that said, "I Flew a B-24," which she pinned
to her stocking cap as she boarded the train for home.

About the Author

Sue Ellen Thompson is the author of five previous books of poetry and the editor of *The Autumn House Anthology of Contemporary American Poetry* (1st ed.). Her work has been included in the *Best American Poetry* series, read more than a dozen times by Garrison Keillor on National Public Radio, and featured in former U.S. Poet Laureate Ted Kooser's nationally syndicated newspaper column. A graduate of Middlebury College and The Bread Loaf School of English, she was a National Arts Club Scholar, a Robert Frost Fellow, and for many years a staff member at The Bread Loaf Writers' Conference. She has taught at Central Connecticut State University, Wesleyan University, Binghamton University, Middlebury, and the University of Delaware. In 1998, she was the resident poet at The Frost Place, Robert Frost's former home in Franconia, New Hampshire.

After spending most of her adult life in Connecticut, she moved to Oxford, Maryland, on the Eastern Shore of the Chesapeake Bay, in 2006. Since then, she has been a mentor to adult poets and an instructor at The Writer's Center in Bethesda, Maryland. In addition to the Samuel French Morse Prize, the Pablo Neruda Prize, a Pushcart Prize, and two Pulitzer Prize nominations, she is the recipient of the 2010 Maryland Author Award, which the Maryland Library Association gives to a poet once every four years for his or her body of work.

www.sueellenthompson.com

CPSIA information can be obtained
at www.ICGtesting.com
Printed in the USA
BVHW080739200122
626620BV00006B/506